Things Change

Joel Landmine

Punk 💣 Hostage 💣 Press

Things Change
© Joel Landmine 2021
ISBN 978-1-940213-14-19

All rights reserved. No part of this book may be used or reproduced in any manner whatsoever without written permission except in the case of brief quotations embodied in critical articles or reviews. For information contact Punk Hostage Press Hollywood, California.

Editor
Iris Berry

Associate Editor & Layout
Michelle McDannold

Foreword
Patrick O'Neil

Cover Design
SB Stokes

Special Thanks
Clinty's bitch ass

Author Photo Courtesy of Joe Carrow

Punk Hostage Press
Hollywood, USA
www.punkhostagepress.com

for Hilda

Contents

Foreword x

Lexical Ambiguity 1

I've Still Got You, Dated Formats 2

Con Safos 3

Wall Street 6

The Fates Are Just Shitty Kids 7

3 PM 8

Untitled for Michael 10

Dystopia #1 12

For John, Who Loves Movies 14

Lemonade 15

Barrio Muerto 16

It Hit Me Just Then 18

Confession #1 19

Bad Circulation 20

The Moment You Said You Loved Me 21

Moat 22

Speculative Fiction 23

Men Are Trash 24

These Bugs Keep Biting Me 26

Confession #3 27

Untitled in the First World 28

John Says	29
Gilda Radner & Gene Wilder	32
Bye Bye Baby Don't Be Blue	33
Windbag Snapshot	34
The Scientific Method	36
Art's Crab Shack Closed	37
Growing Up #1	38
Growing Up #2	39
Growing Up #3	40
Every Political Poem	41
Talking with Dad About Love	42
Serenity Prayer	43
Houdini	44
What It Looks Like	45
Alcoholics Anonymous	48
The MFA	49
It's Hard to Know How to Be	50
Priorities	52
Confession #4	53
Flattery	54
Millenials	55
All Creatures Great and Small	58
Take Good Care of Your Shit	59
Confession #6	60

The Sun Still Sets	62
The Tuesday Before	66
That Second Half	67
Fragment	68
Confession #7	69
Ramen	70
Metaphor #3	72
Species of Least Concern	73
Rejection Hurts	74
IOU	76
Confession #9	77
Death #1	78
Moment of Nostalgia for Old Girlfriends	80
Things Change	81
Two Roads Diverged in a Yellow Wood	82
Inaguruation Day	83
Ten Years Later	84
Death #2	88
Simple Wonders	89
This Poet	90
I've Got the Blues	91
Buzz Buzz Buzz	92
Dust to Dust	94
A Cold Grey Morning in Spring	95

Confession #10	96
You Do What You Can	97
The Green Green Grass of Home	98
People are Dicks #2	99
Dystopia #2	100
March 19th, 2020	102
Death #3	103
When the Shit Goes Down	104

Foreword

Getting asked to write an introduction for another writer is not only an honor, but simultaneously challenging, and complex. My intent is to present them and their new work framed in the context of how I see and feel them. But I also want to make sure the reader understands just how important this writer is to me. It's not just a favor, or an obligation. It's a labor of love and respect. So with that said and before we get any further I'll just straight up tell you. Joel Landmine kicks ass and you need to read his shit right now!

The first time I met Joel was years ago at a reading for Beast Crawl in Oakland, or maybe it was at Joe Clifford's Lip Service West. Either way it doesn't matter. What does is there I was on the side-of-the-stage watching the usual array of writers and poets, while self-obsessed waiting for my turn at the mic. Up walked this skinny dude, pencil thin mustache, a fine ass vintage suit, and he just ripped into poem after poem, deadpan delivery, discarding the pages like used condoms on the killing floor. I thought, *Okay, who the fuck is this motherfucker?* When asked, my wife Jenn said, "That's Joel Landmine." As if I should know better. Now I do.

Yet at that moment, with his disarray of spent poems splayed across the carpet, all that old "I'm too cool for this literary event" peripheral bullshit just ceased to exist. Like everyone else in that room, I was solely focused on Joel as he casually deconstructed the English language with punctilious blasts of .45 caliber prose. None of the usual yahoos in the back were talking shit. A few weren't even breathing. As Joel kept dropping these truncated "Dear John" love-letter eulogies to everything perverse, unholy, and revered. It felt like that first time you saw a missing kid on a milk carton and thought maybe you could aspire to that kind of fame. Or your misaligned sense of accomplishment that last time you came to out of a blackout half-naked on the bathroom floor—sending you that much closer to drinking bad coffee at your first AA meeting. Two lines into his final poem and the rapt silence was punctuated with a collective groan as Joel verbally gut-punched another cultural icon a few of the spectators obviously held sacred. In that dust-settling aftermath this John Waters/Little Richard/Skinny Pete incarnate left the stage completely destroyed. The audience dug it and I was forever sold.

It's safe to say that Joel is a formidable San Francisco Bay Area talent, albeit these days specifically heralding from the East Bay literary scene. As a card-carrying member of that industrious collection of poets and writers Joel is seemingly hell bent on revamping poetry to what it should be. You know, like using language that people can actually identify, and less vague innuendoes of the touchy-feely kind. His work blurs the traditional shared experience between the reader and poet; transcending us into a pathological sing-along where nobody knows the words, but we're still following Joel's bouncing ball.

If you want to read about subversive pop culture, stanky substance abuse, dejected relationships, overt self-depreciation, and the despair of living in a dystopian future, then Joel's your man. He will not disappoint. His first book of poetry *Yeah, Well...* set the tone. Now *Things Change* is going to kick that tone's ass and set the bar even higher. It'd be really lame to announce something like, "Joel Landmine is a poet to keep your eye on as he's going places," because he already left for that higher ground and we're the ones trailing behind.

Patrick O'Neil, author of *Gun, Needle, Spoon*

"Baby, things change."
-*Dwight Yoakam*

"Sometimes people change/ And sometimes that's good/ But sometimes they don't/ When maybe they should."
-*The Supersuckers*

"Sometimes there's a change in the ocean/ Sometimes there's a change in the sea/ Sometimes there's a change in my own true love/ But there's never no change in me"
- *Traditional*

"Things done changed."
-*Biggie*

Lexical Ambiguity

I was 30 years old
before I realized

that when they all talked about their fondness
for Mexican Coke
they meant

the kind that comes in
glass bottles

and not in
the tied-off corners
of discount sandwich bags

I've Still Got You, Dated Formats

I made her two CDs
the day before I broke her heart.
But then the heart-breaking distracted me,
and I forgot to give them to her.

They're still sitting there,
on the shelf above my desk,
collecting dust
in their little paper sleeves,

right next to a tape I made for you
but can never give you,

a letter I can never send.

Con Safos

It's a damn wonder
I didn't get lit up
more often than I did

Once

I had run out of options
so I ended up at this spot
for crackheads off the street
who needed

to stay out of jail
to have something
to show the judge
to show they were trying

There was this big
Fred-Flintstone-ass peckerwood motherfucker there
a terrified child in this hulking man's body
a bully and a coward
like an institutionalized Kevin James

He liked to act hard
but only with weaker men

He never gave me no shit though
always seemed like
he was looking to impress me
But he made me feel sad
he just didn't have no heart

One day we were walking down Duboce
and I said some shit
he wasn't tryna hear

He puffed up real big
started yelling
practically beating his chest
Despite his weak spirit
his fist was about the size of my head

Just when it looked like it was about to go down
I put my face right the fuck up in his
I looked him dead in his eyes

and I said

"You can hit me.
But you can never *hurt* me."

We just stood there
for an endless moment
my face in his
watching his eyes grow

And then
it was like
popping a balloon
with a pin

He seemed to shrink three sizes
or snap out of a trance
all the fire
left his eyes

I'd like to tell you
I said it real quiet
and tough and fierce
but I was scared
I'm just a whisper of a man
and my voice wavered

But that didn't matter though
because we both knew

that I was telling the truth

He muttered
I was just pissed
or something like that

And we just kept walking
chatting like nothing had happened

hurrying a little
to catch the train

Wall Street

I had finally gotten
enough attention that
a couple of poets
had tried to flex nuts.

It caught me off guard,
politics in poetry.
It wasn't something that
had even occurred to me
to prepare myself for.

What is this,
fucking Wall Street?

It seemed to me, this
jockeying for position,
like sabotaging other
checker players
in order to be the best checker player
in the county.

Like, you might even become
the best checker player in the *world*,

 but when it's all said and done,
you were still just playing

fucking checkers.

Sometimes I Think the Fates Are Just Shitty Kids Shoving Firecrackers up Cats' Asses and Lighting Bags of Shit on Fire on People's Stoops

She said she'd go to the ends of the earth,
but she didn't even go to the end of October.

"I have a dentist appointment
tomorrow at one,"
I said.

"Please, *please*, leave before or after that.
Please don't leave me while
I'm sitting at the fucking dentist's,
with those protective glasses
and that little fucking bib, drooling all over myself.
I don't think my heart can bear it."

It was the last thing I ever asked of her.

"Oh *baby*," she cooed
sweetly, kissing my scowling mouth,
"Of *course*. You know I'd never do that to you!"

But

guess what?

3 PM

I wish I could describe
the afternoon light

that comes through
my bedroom window
every day as I read and doze

I wish I could describe
the afternoon light,

gray through the fog
as the washed out
VHS tape of Eraserhead
I watched as a kid

I wish I could describe
the afternoon light,

soft as the skin on your waist,
the skin on the inside of your thighs
near your pussy,
the skin where your neck
meets your shoulder

I wish I could describe
the afternoon light,

quiet as the holding cell
down 850
with the double-paned glass,
once I gave up the banging and the shouting

I wish I could describe
the afternoon light,

comforting as the trains by the freeway going beneath the overpass
and into the tunnel
over and over
again and again

I wish I could describe
the afternoon light,

full moon over the orange groves
for day in the city,
my bed
Cronos' belly

I wish I could describe
the afternoon light,

but perhaps I'm
a lousy poet
or perhaps I just became
a poet too late

Untitled
for Michael French

I've only been busy
for about three years now

I still haven't gotten the hang of it

There are less quiet moments
than there used to be

My bedroom window
opens to another room
in the back of the building
so I can't hear the rain

I miss the sound
and it barely rains anymore anyway

But last night I stood in the kitchen
and peeled a tangerine
and watched the rain
fall on Oakland

          ***

Today I'm helping a friend move
He wanted to get his kids out of East O
so his ex-wife lent him some money
quite a bit in fact
for a down payment on a house

He's late
so I've been sitting here in my car
for a half an hour
just listening

sitting
and listening

to the silence
to the rain
When he gets here

I should thank him

The Despair of Living in the Dystopic Future Looks a Little Different Than I Thought It Might #1

I was hoping
that it would

look more

like Escape From New York
or the
robot wars in The Terminator

and less

like Bed Bath & Beyond
or an
app that finds the nearest Quiznos

but
we do

have the
shrieking liberal word police
on the left

and the
xenophobic open-carry nutjobs with their AR-15s
on the right

and Nancy Grace
yelling at everybody
from 2 billion screens
large and small

So I guess there's that

For John, Who Loves Movies

I thought I
saw you driving
a PT Cruiser down

San Pablo today.
I know that wouldn't be
your first choice

if you could afford a ride,
but it made me realize
how much I miss you.

Lemonade
(Consolation Prize)

We lay in bed that last night,
the sex brought her out
from wherever it is
that she'd been hiding
inside herself

for the past few weeks.

She said
(as a few other
well-meaning assholes
already had),

"Just think of all the great *poems* you'll get out of this!"

"I'd be happy to never write another good poem as long as I live
to just have you here with me.
"Fuck a poem," I said,
"Fuck *poetry*!
I want *you*, fool."

But fuck, man.

She left anyway. So here we are.

Barrio Muerto
(Defector)

During the poetry reading
in the new artisanal soda shop in The Mission
on a block that's had botox,
a block I no longer recognize,
a man with one leg
in madras shorts and a women's cardigan
stopped in the doorway to listen.

A middle-aged woman
in a gold lamé jacket
walked up to him,
her three-year-old daughter
holding her hand.

I saw him palm her cash,
slip her the bag,
a fluid transaction
you'd miss if you
hadn't seen it so many times,

before he started off,
he shouted
"I LOVE YOU, *BABY*!"
at her back,
already most of the way
down the block.

The 49 hissed
as it rolled on down Mission,
I looked back around
at the clean, educated faces inside,

thought about my new job in marketing,
about the diploma I'd worked so hard for
coming in the mail,

remembered that crack park by the McDonald's
across the street from the police station
on Turk & Fillmore,
the breakfasts at Glide Memorial,

and wondered about
the choices I've made.

It Hit Me Just Then, All at Once, That I've Been a Huge Pussy My Entire Life

I saw him,
like the rest of us,
walking with purpose down the hallway.

He carried
a skateboard

in one hand,
for he only had one hand.

His other arm,
the right,
ended just above the elbow.

As he walked,
he carelessly tossed his skateboard

under his right arm,
carrying it with his stump,

never missing a step.

Confession #1

I still want to fuck
stupid women
and horrible women
and stupid and horrible women

and it makes me
fear myself
It makes me
fear men

The idiocy of our desire
Our limitless potential
for folly
for harm

Our incalculable
capacity
for brutality

Bad Circulation

gives you trouble
with the "extremities,"

the fingers, toes,
they get cold,

they lose their feeling.

If it gets bad
enough
they fall off.

1, 2, 3, 4, 5, 6, 7, 8, 9, 10

Soon the extremities
get less extreme.

The hands, the feet.
they fall off, keep chipping away

until the stump ends
at the shoulder, at the thigh,

because the trunk
and the head

got greedy

for all that
precious blood.

From the Moment You Said You Loved Me, All We Did Was Say Goodbye

You was all gravy
       and no potatoes

Moat

"I can't see you guys without my glasses," she said

as she took off her glasses
and looked at us

Speculative Fiction

I'm reading a book about a man
who gets hired on to help this minor god
in a war between the gods.

There's some downtime in this war,
and the minor god
rents the man a little apartment
in a very very cold part of the country

to keep him out of the way,
off the radar.
He gets, this man, a car
and some long underwear and a hot plate.

Since he's the protagonist
and I am the reader
I relate to him,
experience the book through him, right?

And even though it's a compelling book,
and I want to find out what happens,
how this war goes,

between the gods and all,
part of me
just wants him to stay forever
alone in his rented apartment, alone with some books

and the hot plate
and the cold outside
because that just
sounds so good.

Men Are Trash

The woman collecting the beer glasses
saw me looking at her
and scowled as though she had
caught me fantasizing
about
having sex with her

I can understand
Her top
was low cut
and I imagine she
gets that a lot

It must get mad irritating
when you're
just trying to get the rent paid
just trying to get through
your shift

But she'd actually
caught me fantasizing
about
what she'd look like
without any hair on her head

It's incredible
how much
someone's hair
can change their appearance

I still diverted my gaze
looked away
a little ashamed

as I would have
had she been right

These Bugs Keep Biting Me

I never see them,
but I'm covered in the bites.

I've always reacted badly to bug bites,
itch like a son-of-a-bitch,
and they've always loved to bite me,

ever since I was a kid.
The itching reminds me

of how I felt inside,
in those months
after she left.

It's excruciating

just to leave them,
but I scratch them
bloody and swollen

when I don't.
Except now,

when you rub the cream
on the ones on my back
that I can't reach,

I'm here with you, as I
could just never be then.

Confession #3
(Why This Shit is here on the Floor)

It is too cold
and there are too many rats
by the dumpster
to take out the trash tonight

I am scared of the cold
I am scared of the rats

And so this bag
of my cats' shit
that I've so diligently dug up
with my special little shovel

will sit here on
the kitchen floor

overnight

Untitled Poem about Life in the First World at the Dawn of the New Millennium

As they walked past hand in hand,
I overheard the child, petulant, say
to his mother

"Mom, I want more…

SOMETHING."

Welcome to the rest of your life,
kid.

John Says
for John Panzer

My friend told me
"No one will play my game
of 'I'm a writer so I get to be a drug addict.'

I kind of wanted to get away with that."
I understood exactly what he meant.

When I was younger
I read a lot of books
about descents into madness.

They always sounded
romantic to me,

I liked punk records
and Hank Williams too,
that sort of thing.

But then I had me one once,
a descent into madness,

a few, actually.

***

Once I had been up for three days and
thought I was
covered head to toe
in fleas. I got in the bath
(the fleas *hate* the water, I thought)

but I was too tall to be fully submerged.

If I put my head under,
my knees stuck out,
and I could feel them rushing
madly for the peaks.

When I put my knees under,
my head stuck out
and I could feel them stampeding between the follicles
for the top of my head.

***

Another time
I spent a week locked up in a shitbag motel room,
too depressed to answer the phone
because I couldn't stand to hear the sound

of my own voice,
bugs, real bugs this time, biting me in my sleep,
just trying to stay drunk enough
not to take a bus to the bridge.

There was this whole TV show
where shallow women stabbed each other
in the back for a
chance to sleep with
the singer from a 1980s hair-metal band.

Not him in 1988, him *now*.
That week the only thing on TV was a marathon of this show.
When you've lost all faith in humankind
that ain't the kind of thing that'll bring you on back.

***

"Listen, John," I said into the telephone,
"this whole descent-into-madness thing,
I've tried it, man.
And they just don't live how they read,
you know?"

Gilda Radner & Gene Wilder

You know how couples
sometimes talk in bed a little
before they go to sleep at night?

I bet they were the best at that.

Bye Bye Baby, Don't Be Blue

While peeing
I blew a spider
off of a porcelain clown
and out the open window.

For a moment
it made me feel
like a God.

A casually angry, vengeful God,
reveling in the arbitrary violence
and senseless chaos

of a world I'd created by accident,
and had long lost any
real control over.

Windbag Snapshot

I took the three freeways
and dropped her off
at beauty school
my eyes still crusted with sleep

I returned home
it was still
early morning
a chill overcast
morning in August

I sat down at
my desk in
my dark bedroom
the lamp so dim I could barely see
and looked down at the UPS slip

They can't leave packages
by the door here
they'll get stolen
And they never
come by when you're home

The slip says
that today
will be their "Final Attempt"
it sounds so menacing

I don't trust them
so on the back
on the line marked "Signature"

I write "Please Ring"
and on the line marked "Print Name"
I write "doorbell"

I sat there in the semidarkness and
squinted at the lines
I had gotten ash all over the
adhesive strip
on the side of the slip

I'm a grown man,
but I still have the handwriting of a child
and something about the misuse
of the official lines
to scrawl this little message

there was lewd poetry in it
these little moments
they happen all day long
they pass all day long
all the little signs
on all the businesses
out the window of the bus

As I walked down the stairs
hoping the slip would still stick to the door

I thought
"I should write this down

so I don't lose it
like all the others…"

The Scientific Method
(People Are Dicks and I'm No Different #1)

I had to go see about a thing
so there would be no doubt

when it came back around

to you

Art's Crab Shack Closed the Other Day, and Kaplan's Is Long Gone

"People aren't poor because there isn't enough money."
-Jon the Bus Driver

When the proverbial canary
ate dirt in the proverbial coal mine
the miners had the good sense
to kick rocks

But these canaries keep fuckin' dying
and we all just sit around
going, "Man, that sucks.
I really *liked* that canary!"

and waiting to
get evicted
waiting to
choke on the fumes

Growing Up #1

I was in love with her

    not with

        the idea of her

Growing Up #2

I hated the band Journey
for most of my life.

Then I was dating this young girl,
kind of a laid-back beach babe with a rough past.

We were riding in her car one day,
and Don't Stop Believing came on.

"How can you *listen* to this shit?"
I asked.

She said, simply, confidently,
"Because it makes me feel good."

In that moment,
decades of snobbery and judgement fell away.

After that I stopped being such an asshole
a little bit.

I still hate fuckin' Journey,
but I try to be careful

not to begrudge anyone
anything that brings them joy

Growing Up #3

I had ten days off of work,
and I went to Target,
and then to Safeway,

and now it's over.

Every Political Poem
for G Macías Gusman and for all the mediocre slam poets

Things
could probably be better

Things
could definitely be better

I
could even tell you how

Talking with Dad About Love

I loved all my wives he said
I loved them all

When you were three years old
I told you I really love Freddy

You looked up at me and said

Well she sure don't love you

three years old

He took a bite of his steak
You were always a smart kid
he said

Serenity Prayer

There's ants in my kitchen
and bullets on my block

The ants drive me crazy
the shots I pay no mind

because dammit
I should be able to *do* something
about these ants

Houdini

Poor bastard.

Cheated death all those times,
and finally caught it

behind some dumbass
party trick.

Ain't that the way it is.

What It Looks Like

We went to the bank and added my name
to an old account of hers
so we could start to save up money
to get a place of our own

Her ex was still on the account
I found out his deadname
from when he had still been
living as a woman when the teller inquired

When she said
"Oh! That's my ex!"
the teller in his dapper little Macy's suit
saw the look of surprise on my face at hearing a women's name

and looked nervous
almost breaking a sweat
though it was a cold rainy day in December
He realized too late

that he'd disclosed
some information that
I wasn't supposed to know
though it wasn't the information he thought it was

A young woman in scrubs
speaking to a banker in the cubicle next to ours
was trying to sort out her credit card
also had an ex-boyfriend

"And I was doing so *well!*"
I heard her say

***

We lay in bed that night when I got off work
We'd cancelled our obligations
so we could watch our program

We stopped it to have sex
but I came so fast
trying to stop myself
even after it was over
that we didn't have the chance to really enjoy it

But afterward we laughed about it
Not the awkward this-has-never-happened-to-me-before laughter
but with genuine warmth and amusement

We watched our show
and read a dubiously written article
about the qualities couples in lasting marriages have
We laughed about the suspect nature of the writing

but we were both secretly
smug and pleased
that we saw ourselves falling
on the right side of the cited studies

***

She fell asleep and as I read
she woke for a moment
just a few minutes later

Without sitting up
she said
that she'd had a dream
that a man was hitting on her
wasn't picking up her hints
that she wasn't interested

"He put his arm around my shoulder"
she said
sleepy and sweet and proud
"so I bit his hand!"

I couldn't see her face
but I could hear her smile
as she drifted back off

Alcoholics Anonymous

These two dudes
both raised their hands
and spoke about
how spiritual they each were

Then
after the meeting
they fought each other
in the parking lot

The MFA

Before the interminable explanation
of the piece he was about to read,

he laughed nervously and said,
"I'm a firm believer in the rules."

I think that he thought that he was making a joke,

but

we all believed him,
with all our hearts.

It's Hard to Know How to Be

I try hard,
to be a good man,
to be a stand-up dude.

Equality is important to me,
I read and think about society,
my place in it,
the arbitrary advantages I was born into,
try to incorporate it in the way I live.

But I'm a deeply flawed person
and it's a fucked up, messy world.
There are so many conflicting messages,
all these little lessons,

arguing with each other,
competing with one another for attention,
and it's hard to know
how to be.

***

I used to know this woman. "Harder!" she yelled at me, furiously rubbing her clit. I was slamming my cock into her asshole, fucking her the way I imagined a hyena might. As she came, her whole body shook, the way the house shook during Loma Prieta back in '89, down to her foundations.

As soon as she'd finished,
she collapsed into tears,
wild, anguished sobs.
I stopped fucking, mortified.

I loved her. But she was still in love with another man, so I hadn't told her that. I don't think I ever did, though I'm certain that it showed.

And she was clearly in pain.
The bad kind,
not the sexy kind.
I was worried for her wellbeing, my instinct to comfort her.

I mean, I like it hard and everything, I'm a pervert, sure, but I'm not a fucking psychopath. I don't know, maybe I'm square, but pain can be sexy, real *suffering* not so much.

She looked at me over shoulder,
eyes filled with contempt,

like I was the biggest sissy she'd ever met,
and said, "Why are you stopping?"

Priorities
(You Can't Get What You Want If You Don't Know What You Want)

I knew this retired bus driver
had severe diabetes

He'd lost half a foot
the other leg from the thigh down
had gone completely blind

but
54 years married
all he wanted from his doctor

was more Viagra

Confession #4

It's alarming
how thin my wrists are

I used to wear spikes
like a sea urchin
like a porcupine
to try to convince the world
that I was to be left the fuck alone

but the bracelets never came small enough
for my thin wrists
so the heavy leather bands
with their studs and spikes
rattled around

more bangles
than cuffs

I look at them
my thin wrists
they embarrass me
make me feel insecure

I imagine that a stronger man
or fierce woman
could probably snap them
without too much effort

Thankfully
it's never come to that

Flattery

There is a certain type
of person
who has heard

the perhaps backhanded,
but most deeply heartfelt
compliment

that one
can expect
to hear.

"I'm so glad
you didn't
kill yourself."

The Old World is Gone Forever
(Millennials)

People say that they're lazy
but I don't know.

Most of them
seem to have more hustle
than I ever did.

But still
it makes me so sad
to know that
most of them

will never know
the simple,
utter
satisfactions

of

slamming the phone receiver
angrily
into its cradle

or

the sound
of throwing a proper television
off of the roof
of a building.

My Heart Was Wrapped Up in Clovers
for Kelly

She mentioned *At Last,*
she said "I know, I know
it's a played-out wedding song,
but I'm just so
partial to Etta."

"The weddings I've done," I said, "and maybe
it's just the type of people
that ask me to DJ their weddings,
but that's by far my number one wedding request. With a bullet."

She went back to her planning book,
she was asking me
about something else,
but I was distracted.

I was at our wedding,
imagining standing up there,
hearing those first string notes,
seeing her emerge from the back in her dress
with her flowers, her dad, that *moment*…

I couldn't even imagine it that good.
We still didn't know where it would be,
what we would wear,
exactly what day it would be,

but just thinking about that moment,
sitting there outside the coffee shop
at dusk on a Tuesday night,

drinking our coffees and smoking and talking
like we always do after work,

just *thinking* about it,
I had to hold back the tears of
gratitude and joy
that were welling up behind my eyes.

"Maybe something else," I laughed,
"Maybe pick another song.
I don't think I wanna cry during the ceremony
in front of all our friends."

In the end
she picked an Elvis song,
and no one was surprised
when my voice cracked a little
anyway.

All Creatures Great and Small

Looking out my window
I saw

a butterfly
and a jetliner

Take Good Care of Your Shit

In every city I've ever lived in,
at any time of the day or night,
there is always

always

a bum
furiously sweeping
some small patch of it.

I have mad respect for that dude.

All them dudes.

Confession #6

The day we bought our wedding rings
it rained and rained.
I dozed on the couch
and looked out at it

thought about how nice it would be
not to go outside
thought on the drive
the windshield wipers working their hardest
about smoking weed
what that used to feel like

We went to the place I'd heard
in the radio commercials
my whole life long
even joked about it with the salesman
who seemed too young
to have ever listened to the radio

Afterward she went to the office supply store
next door to the jeweler in the strip mall
She loves stationery and pens and little containers
She seemed as excited
about the clipboard she picked out

as she did about the diamonds
I think the extravagance of the jewelry store
with all its thousand-dollar trinkets
caused her anxiety
embarrassed her

called attention to our
modest little lives
and the familiarity of the brightly lit chain store
provided relief

We went home
and I cooked her fish for dinner
She doesn't like it
but it suited the diet she was on
which was fine by me

We watched TV
and went to bed and
read and read
neither of us could sleep

I went into the kitchen
and got a leftover pork chop
ate it standing
cold from the fridge
and thought about how far I've come

all the skills I've learned
all these things I know
but how
well into manhood
I've still not learned to make a living
and realized how deeply scared I am
that I never really will

The Sun Still Sets Every Night, Even When the Sunset Doesn't Take Your Breath Away, Even When You Don't Even Notice It

I used to write lines about "your heart
beating so close to mine"
and nonsense like that.

I was so sure
that a life without you would be
unbearable.
But what the fuck do you know,
I bore it.

I thought of you briefly the other day, and was surprised to find
that I couldn't give less of a shit where you were, who you were with,
really even about any thought
you ever have.

No malice either,
just no regard.
My heart didn't flutter,
my stomach didn't sink.
It was equivalent,
emotionally,
to thinking of a restaurant I'd been to once or twice
that I thought was pretty alright.
Not great, not bad,
just pretty alright,

just like "Oh yeah. That one place is there."

But what you thought
used to RULE me.
Dictated my behavior, my decisions, obsessing, futilely trying
to be the made-up man I thought you'd have me be,
the deepest kind of joy when it seemed like I was,
the deepest kind of pain when you decided I wasn't.

But now just nonchalance.

I mean,
how does that even *happen*?

***

There's this song "Good Woman" by this singer Cat Power
It's real maudlin if you're not in it
but real poignant if you are
like that one Adele song that was so popular a few years back

I remember the first time I heard it
I'd lost everything,
everything in my life
that I gave half a shit about

Like, it was two years
before I even
reached that point
we so casually call "starting over"

Of course

"everything"
included a woman

So I took all that loss
and put it in that woman's purse
and hung that purse
from a penny nail that I drove through my own heart
hung it from that song

But that was a long time ago
I was a youngblood
didn't know any different
any better

But now
the downstairs neighbor keeps playing it

so loud I can hear it
through the windows
through the floor

just over and over
again
all morning
all night

I want to go down there
put my hand on their shoulder
tell them that it's gonna be ok
that it's not always gonna hurt like this
tell them "Come on,

you've gotta stop *doing* this to yourself."

But nobody
talks
to their neighbors anymore

Noon on the Tuesday Before I Got Married

Covered with old scars
They still itch from time to time
and maybe they look kinda ugly

But fuck it

They've all healed up
OK enough
and today I feel just fine

The Second Half of the Second Decade of the Twenty First Century

Prince died the day before we got married
and though our love was strong

the whole world just kept getting worse after that

Fragment from the Monthly Reading at the Karaoke Bar

"Give yourself over to laughter,"
the nervous woman

with the trendy asymmetric
haircut
who

didn't seem like she laughed very much
said
half into the microphone

as the little boy
with the deformed face
broke into a grin

on the television screen
above the bar

Confession #7

All things considered,
if I'm really being honest,
at the end of the day

I was not a wild man.

I was too afraid.

Ramen

It's Thursday afternoon,
and I'm picking clean
the carcass of a chicken I bought Monday night,
to put the meat in my ramen.

I've been writing for a company
that's run out
of money. But we've set ourselves up
in the meantime

to have a very successful
year. In the next week

we will either get a check from
a new customer and get back on our feet,

or we won't.
And we'll go under.
I'll still be broke,
but unemployed on top of it.

The suspense,
the stakes,
are making it hard to get up,
hard to concentrate.

But today
I am grateful.

It wasn't so long ago,
and it might well not be long again,
that there was no chicken at all
for the ramen.

Metaphor #3

Sometimes my cigarette sticks to my lip,
and tears away a tiny piece of skin.

For a few days afterward it stings, just a little bit,
and I compulsively flick it
with my tongue,

which makes it sting a little bit more.
But just a little bit.

It would go away faster if I left it alone,
and it's kind of annoying.
But there's something I like about it.

Species of Least Concern
for Paul Corman Roberts

Every few years
some expert declares
that poetry is dead

The fool!

Be it gentle or violent
as long as the rain still falls
as long as hearts still break open
there will always be poets

Rejection Hurts, Even Though the People That Love Us Do the Best They Know How

They were friends
but he seemed to regard her,
a little older,
as a mother or a governess,

he was full of admiration and affection,
but clearly craved her approval,
I had watched her straighten his tie in the parking
lot earlier that night.

They read together,
and as they left the podium smiling,
he, much taller than her,
reached to hold her hand,

but she didn't see,
and walked past him,
so as not to block the aisle.

He kept walking behind,
didn't break stride,
but just for a fleeting second,
I saw on his face

the sting of embarrassment,
of rejection,

like when you smile and wave,

only to realize a moment too late
that they'd been waving

at someone behind you.

IOU

Every time
I hear your name

my heart
swells

with gratitude
with indebtedness

and I raise my face up toward God in praise
and I solemnly thank fuckin' Christ

that you
left me

Confession #9
(and Advice for Lost Young People)

I don't know
what to do.

Like, I have
no fucking idea what to do.

Not just right now, today,
but all the time.

Really, I've *never* known what to do.

I mean if I see someone
and ask about their weekend
and they say,
"Oh, it was fun! We went up to the river!"
I always think,
"Like… How did you know to do that?"

But shit, man.

All this stuff happened,
and I had this whole life anyway.
It just happens.

Ever Since We Been Sentient We Been Trying to Figure Out How to Deal With Death but We Just Haven't Yet #1

We were watching television
when we got the call that her grandfather was dead.
He'd been ailing a long time,
we'd been back and forth
from Stockton for weeks.

Her mother, her aunt, and his wife had
been eating dinner.
When they were finished, they went
to wake him up, but he was finally done
waking up.

He knew, and he was ready,
had been ready.
I'd heard him deliver his own eulogy
months before,
before he really turned.

His wife, sweet with dementia,
sat and talked to his body.
She wasn't ready to say goodbye.

Her mother said over the phone
that the Neptune Society
would come and get his body, and they'd
burn it up,
and that would be that.
That's what she said,
that would be that.

She cried for a while,
and we talked,
and we watched some more of the television show.

She sent me out for candy,
when I came home she was asleep on the couch.
I sat with her and ate some candy,
while a bank of servers,
each 10,000 times more powerful
than the most powerful fucking super-computer
the year of my birth,

beamed a movie with Marilyn Monroe
and Robert Mitchum

that I'd never seen before
right into our damn living room.

What a thing,
just to live.

Moment of Nostalgia for Old Girlfriends

With the sun high
and the shadows long

I watched a moth
fight a bee on
a windowsill.

The bee got bored
and left.

Things Change

My wife got this
new coffee maker
It's a beautiful piece of machinery
that brews one fresh cup at a time
with these tiny reusable filters

She loves it
It's objectively better than the old one

on every level
but shit man
I miss the sputtering sound of the percolator
and my pots
of shitty coffee

Two Roads Diverged in a Yellow Wood

I meant to ask you
what's up with your friend

but that was hella years ago
and I'm married now

Inauguration Day

The day Trump,
that cartoon parody of a rich guy from my childhood,
that buffoonish crybaby racist demagogue,
that impossibly absurd combination of silly and sinister,
that final proof that there really is no limit to American incompetence,
that harbinger of suffering and likely annihilation,
was inaugurated

we could feel the doom in the air,

and my wife and I went to the grocery store
in the pouring rain.
When we came out,
the downpour continued as we ran to try to keep
our brown paper bags
from getting soggy.

But the sun had peeked through,
and stretching across the sky
was the most vivid and glorious
double rainbow
that either of us
had ever seen.

The next day
millions
across the nation
took to the streets.

But he just started doing what he was gonna do anyway.

Ten Years Later

The damp last-ditch drug program by the sea
with its sagging ceilings
and the black mold on the walls

Grown men in their thirties and forties
constantly
bitching and bickering
acting like hard men
but sounding like
school children in need of a nap
because nobody
had ever showed them how
to act right

more a flophouse
than a treatment center

I'd been there for 30 days
and was finally allowed to leave by myself
unsupervised

I went downtown
and bought two bottles of Nyquil
and went to a movie theater
to watch a movie
about Russian gangsters

I sat in the darkened theater
and drank both bottles
as though they were shots

I figured I'd get a little buzz on
and watch my movie
and go back there

without stinking of booze
without anyone being the wiser

For once
everything went as planned

It was the last drink
I ever had

***

Ten years later
on the same night
I feared for my home

they were selling my building
and my wife and I couldn't afford to move
I hated my job
wasn't sure I could do it
and it was really important that I do it
I was swamped and I needed the check

Someone dented my car
I found an abscess in my mouth
Much of the country was on fire or underwater
as people I loved

came to celebrate this milestone
We went to my favorite place
They got me chicken and greens and iced tea

The waitress
20 years past her prime with a mouthful of gold
blew us all away
with the most soulful rendition of Happy Birthday
any of us had ever heard

I was moved
wondered to myself why she wasn't famous
why she was a waffle waitress and not a singer
until she hugged me
and I smelled the Malibu on her breath
and I understood
and I fleetingly thought

about how if things
had gone the other way
for me probably nobody would even
let me serve waffles

Despite the love
despite all the triumphs
I felt sad and somehow defeated

I was nearing the end of the second week
of intense depression
on the heels of a year
of slightly less intense depression

But I thought of Raymond Carver
How in his tenth year sober
he found gratitude
in the face of death

And I listened to the new Jay-Z
and marveled at how even a person with everything
can grow and grow and grow
And how Biggie didn't have that chance
and everything he could have given us all

And I put on the movie
about the Russian gangsters
and wrote this down

Ever Since We Been Sentient We Been Trying to Figure Out How to Deal With Death but We Just Haven't Yet #2

One time I was pressured to do a favor for this dude
but I didn't
because I never liked his ass

and now he's dead
and it's making me feel a feeling
which I can't identify

but it's not guilt
and it's not regret
so I don't know what to tell you

This World is Chock Full of Simple Wonders

I stopped folding laundry for a second and
just stood
and watched this kitten
drinking water from his bowl
and thought
Shit man
there's just so much
I don't know anything about

I Would Much Rather Once Again Taste the Putrid Geyser of Pus that Erupted When My Swollen, Abscessed Jaw Burst Inside My Mouth at the Dental ER That One Time Than Listen to This Poet Say One More Goddam Word

He was the nails
on the chalkboard

of my comfort
of my tolerance
of the hard-won

goodwill toward mankind I've been
painstakingly cultivating all these years

Just to survive
the 3 minutes he read

without doing
something I'd regret

I scribbled this poem
on the program for

the reading
and then he was done

gone from my life
for what I hoped

would be forever

I've Got the Blues
(and I Just Can't Be Satisfied)

Tonight I saw this dude sitting in his car in the Safeway parking lot
straight chugging a jar of roasted peanuts
the way you would chug a 40

He looked like he
barely made it out the door
before he popped those suckers

I don't know what his story is
but I know that kind
of insatiability

Apparently
peanuts
are all he has left

Buzz Buzz Buzz

I'm barely 40
and my back
is fucked already

I thought it would be good
to take a bath

We have this big old
claw foot tub
but there's only a showerhead
no spigot

So I run the shower
boil a stockpot worth of water
but when I get in there
it's still too cold
to be worth a shit

But I just sit in there anyway
reading a book
in the lukewarm bath just listening
to the noise from the freeway from the city from my head

My wife comes home from work
finds me in there
she goes and gets a salad bowl
from the kitchen

pours bowlfuls of hot water
until the temperature's better
and leaves
to meet a friend for coffee

I put down the book
and sink my ears
my head
beneath the water

Dust to Dust

They say we're all
gonna be just dirt in the ground
dust in the wind

But I read somewhere
that we replace all our cells
every seven years

and that most house dust
is 70 or 80 percent
human skin
We're constantly shedding

So all of us
except the very young
are mostly dust

already anyway

A Cold Grey Morning in Spring

I'm supposed to be thinking
the boring creative thoughts
that they pay me to think
but they're not coming so

I guess I'll stop staring
at this monitor for a minute
and put in a load of laundry
and keep not accepting

this Facebook friend request
from my grandma

Confession #10
(Store in a Cool, Dark Place)

For all those years
all I did
was work and drink

but what I loved most was

to stay up late
and sleep all day

But then
I got my shit together

got a degree
bought a car
got married
built my credit
and destroyed it again
we're talking about kids
and people tell me I should teach

But I'm terrified
that they will find out

that what I love the most is

still

to stay up late
and sleep all day

You Do What You Can

I used to know
this guy

I tried to help him
with his drinking problem
but I couldn't so

now I just
send him the beautiful photos I take
of the flat dead things

I find on the street
around the city

It's Good to See the Green Green Grass of Home
(Things are Tough All Over)

2000 miles from home
got a car in Memphis

crossed Elvis Presley Boulevard
and pulled onto that old 61 Highway

And there
by the side of the road

was a busted-ass Church's Chicken
just like the one
around the corner from my building

Everybody is Judging All the Time, Even When They Tell You Not to, Even When They Don't Even Know They're Doing It
(People are Dicks and I'm No Different #2)

His two smaller toes ended
where the two larger toes began.

There was something obscene about it,
far more disturbing and grotesque
than any true disfigurement.

If I had feet like that, I thought,
I would never,
never ever,
wear Birkenstocks
out in public.

Then again,
I would never,
never ever,
wear Birkenstocks
out in public

anyway,
so…

The Despair of Living in the Dystopic Future Looks a Little Different Than I Thought It Might #2

I wrote this poem
a few years back that
seems hopelessly naive now
in its innocent cynicism

It was about how
I'd hoped that being alive for the space-aged future
would look more like
it had in all those movies

Now

the robots have started to
actually kill people
And the robots have figured out
that it's more efficient to

just turn the humans against one another
and let us do the killing ourselves
or otherwise tear ourselves apart
tear each other apart

But listen
The evil robots aren't even
the worst of it
not even fuckin' close

***

At this point

it's starting to look like
kind of a
monkey's paw type deal

I wished for chaos

    and chaos came

        I'm sorry

March 19th, 2020

I got off the graveyard got home around 8
sat on the stairs in the back by the onramp
and looked at the news on my phone
The virus had spread

Travel was barred two weeks
or two months too late nobody knew
they just knew it was too late
Nobody could go to work

When a day or two off already meant
being out on the street
When the tent cities were already too full to hold
any more on the street

The Dow Jones fell two thousand points in a day

I watched two blackbirds
gathering brush in their mouths
to make a nest

Ever Since We Been Sentient We Been Trying to Figure Out How to Deal With Death but We Just Haven't Yet #3

So my father is a doctor who was totally unable to accept his wife's impending and certain death, who was willing to do anything to keep her alive. He was successful. She lived literally years longer than expected, through not one but at least a dozen almost certainly fatal complications.

The day after she died, we turned on the television.
"What movie is this?" he asked.
"It's The Brain That Wouldn't Die," I said. It's about a doctor who, unable to accept his fiancée's impending and certain death, keeps her head alive in a lab and kills young women to try to transplant her disembodied head onto.

I held his hand in mine.
"I know you would have if you could have, Dad," I said.

When the Shit Goes Down and They Finally Come for Me

Do with me
as y'all will

but I got to eat Häagen-Dazs
and watch old reruns of Cheers
on the couch
next to my sleeping wife and cats
on a cool fall night

and nobody can ever
take that from me

Joel Landmine *lives and works in Oakland California with his wife and cats. This is his second collection of poetry. His first book,* Yeah, Well…, *received a five star Amazon review from some dude who also gave a five star review to a 24-count box of Charleston Chews. So his poems are as good or better than a 24-count box of Charleston Chews. According to some guy in Utah.*

MORE ABOUT THE AUTHOR

"The Henny Youngman of poetry."

    -S.A. Griffin, *Dreams Gone Mad with Hope*

"Joel Landmine's poetry is full of the raw energy one finds in punk music and art but it is also informed by a keen literary and historical sensibility that acts as a foil to the adrenaline and bluster. Both immediate and meditative, vehement and melancholy, this collection offers the reader a conversation and a challenge to look inward. A thoroughly enjoyable, thought provoking and emotionally rich book."

    -Jesse Michaels, *Whispering Bodies*, Operation Ivy

Sometimes you need a poet to remind you of what life is really about. When you read these poems, you'll get the feeling Joel Landmine didn't sign up to be that poet, but thank goodness he stepped up to the task anyway. Landmine tells you exactly how he's feeling and exactly how things are when it comes to feeling like crap, growing up, staying sober, and more. Reading his words, I laughed out loud, I cursed out loud, and I wondered out loud how he nails down those seemingly unspeakable parts of life with such raw honesty. He might shit on your favorite band or your former relationships or your "dapper little Macy's suit," but in the end, you'll thank him for it. You'll thank him for every word.

    -Maisha Z. Johnson, *No Parachutes to Carry Me Home*, *Everyday Feminism*

"Joel Landmine grows up in THINGS CHANGE. The early poems tell of his falling down into love before eventually rising up to confirm his heart's desire for congruent intimacy. The rough integrity of his voice and vision is a joy to track throughout this collection of poems that veers very close to a memoir-in-verse. I encourage you to read his poetry and delight in the gritty magic of his observations on life and nearness to ourselves."

    -Joe Loya, *The Man Who Outgrew His Prison Cell, The Score: Bank Robber Diaries*

"You know those vegetarians who don't like vegetables, only eat bread and cheese? Joel is like the poet of that."

    -Bucky Sinister, *Black Hole*, The Business SF

"The simplicity of these poems hides the weight of what's underneath them."

    -Josiah Luis Alderette, Poet, Taquero, Radio Personality

MORE ABOUT THE AUTHOR

"[Landmine's work sounds like] the diary of a sixteen-year-old-girl [sic] as written by a thirtysomething hipster sitting in front of some records imagining he's being real when actually he's a self-indulgent douche who's never allowed himself to understand shit."

    -Anonymous Internet Commenter

"This witty collection is a little bit Tom Waits and a little bit Dorothy Parker. Some of the ironic titles are as good as the poems themselves and the poems are good: economical and hard-hitting. Landmine's voice is real and authentic, whether waxing philosophical or cracking wise."

    -Natasha Dennerstein, *About a Girl*, *Triptych Caliform*

"Joel Landmine in *Things Change* shows readers what it's like to grow as 'a deeply flawed person [in this] fucked up, messy world. There are so many conflicting messages, all these little lessons, arguing with each other, competing with one another for attention, and it's hard to know how to be,' but in this collection of work I get a glimpse of all of the things that molded Joel Landmine into an artist that I admire in the same vein as John Waters and Harmony Korine. This work is a quintessential collection that shows us how to write ourselves into a cannon that allows us to be both individual, and, oh so, raw and relatable"

    -Vernon Keeve III , *Southern Migrant Mixtape*, Educator

"Sorry Joel, you've reached the wrong Caitlin."

    -Caitlin Meyer, *The Christmas Project*, *Christmas Oranges*, *Christmas Project Reunion*

"You think you know what to expect from these poems. Tough guy poems. You think he's gonna romanticize the gutter. But the romance is in a UPS slip. A spider in the bathroom. A surprise, joyous love in a strip mall office supply store. His work begins with the mundane and then opens out to something much bigger. You'll be laughing at the MFA dude at a poetry reading and never see it coming, swift as a blade, your heart breaks open."

    -Caitlin Myer, *Wiving: A Memoir of Loving Then Leaving the Patriarchy*

"A testament to how far we've come, how shitty we still can be, and how truly beautiful the world is with us in it, these poems help us survive."

    -Tomas Moniz, *Rad Dad* Zine, Teacher

MORE PUNK HOSTAGE PRESS BOOKS

Fractured (2012) by Danny Baker

By A. Razor
Better Than a Gun in a Knife Fight (2012)
Drawn Blood: Collected Works From D.B.P.LTD., 1985-1995 (2012)
Beaten Up Beaten Down (2012)
Small Catastrophes in a Big World (2012)
Half-Century Status (2013).
Days of Xmas Poems (2014)
Puro Purismo (2021)

By Iris Berry
The Daughters of Bastards (2012)
All That Shines Under the Hollywood Sign (2019)

Impress (2012) by C.V. Auchterlonie

Tomorrow, Yvonne - Poetry & Prose for Suicidal Egoists (2012) by Yvonne De la Vega

Miracles of the Blog: A Series (2012) by Carolyn Srygley-Moore

8th & Agony (2012) by Rich Ferguson

By Jack Grisham
Untamed (2013)
Code Blue: A Love Story ~ Limited Edition (2014)
Code Blue: The Hide Under the Mattress Edition (2020)

By Dennis Cruz
Moth Wing Tea (2013)
The Beast Is We (2018)

Blood Music (2013) by Frank Reardon

Showgirl Confidential (2013) by Pleasant Gehman

MORE PUNK HOSTAGE PRESS BOOKS

Yeah, Well... (2014) by Joel Landmine

Stealing the Midnight from a Handful Of Days (2014)
by Michele McDannold

History of Broken Love Things (2014) by SB Stokes *Dreams Gone Mad*

With Hope (2014) by S.A. Griffin

How To Take a Bullet and Other Survival Poems (2014)
by Hollie Hardy

Dead Lions (2014) by A.D. Winans

By Nadia Bruce-Rawlings
Scars (2014)
Driving in the Rain (2020)

WHEN I WAS A DYNAMITER, Or, How a Nice Catholic Boy Became a Merry Prankster, a Pornographer, and a Bridegroom Seven Times (2014)
by Lee Quarnstrom

By Alexandra Naughton
I Will Always Be Your Whore/Love Songs for Billy Corgan (2014)
You Could Never Objectify Me More Than I've Already Objectified Myself (2015)

No Parachutes to Carry Me Home (2015) by Maisha Z Johnson

#1 Son and Other Stories (2017) by Michael Marcus

LOOKING FOR JOHNNY, The Legend of Johnny Thunders (2018) by Danny Garcia

Burden of Concrete (2020) by William S. Hayes

Dillinger's Thompson (2020) by Todd Moore

$100-A-Week Motel by Dan Denton 2021

www.ingramcontent.com/pod-product-compliance
Lightning Source LLC
Chambersburg PA
CBHW020941090426
42736CB00010B/1225